STREAMING

OTHER BOOKS BY
ALLISON ADELLE HEDGE COKE

POETRY
Blood Run
Dog Road Woman
Off-Season City Pipe

MEMOIR
Rock Ghost, Willow, Deer

ANTHOLOGY EDITOR
Effigies
Effigies II
Sing: Poetry of the Indigenous Americas

For the first year of release, a free download of the *Streaming* album
recordings with Rd Klā is available with the purchase of this book.
Enter the code: fH6k7NmR at soundtrax.com to receive.
It is also available for purchase. Please see rdkla.com
or allisonadellehedgecoke.com for information.

Streaming

POEMS

Allison Adelle Hedge Coke

COFFEE HOUSE PRESS

2014

Copyright © 2014 Allison Adelle Hedge Coke
Cover and book design by Linda Koutsky
Cover photo © Melissa Groo (melissagroo.com)
Author photo © Shane Brown

Coffee House Press books are available to the trade through our pri-
mary distributor, Consortium Book Sales & Distribution, cbsd.com
or (800) 283-3572. For personal orders, catalogs, or other information,
write to: info@coffeehousepress.org.

Coffee House Press is a nonprofit literary publishing house. Sup-
port from private foundations, corporate giving programs, government
programs, and generous individuals helps make the publication of our
books possible. We gratefully acknowledge their support in detail in
the back of this book.

Visit us at coffeehousepress.org.

LIBRARY OF CONGRESS CIP INFORMATION

Hedge Coke, Allison Adelle.
[Poems. Selections]
Streaming / Allison Adelle Hedge Coke.
pages cm
ISBN 978-1-56689-375-6 (paperback)
ISBN 978-1-56689-383-1 (ebook)
I. Title.
PS3553.O4366A6 2014
811'.54—DC23
2014008087

PRINTED IN THE UNITED STATES OF AMERICA
24 23 22 21 20 19 18 17   3 4 5 6 7 8 9 10

FOR MY MOTHER
FOR OUR WORLD

PRELUDE

A TIME
elegy for my mother

The problem—
it's not been written yet, the omens:
the headless owl, the bobcat struck,
the red wolf where she could not be.

None of it done and yet it's over.

Nothing yet
of night   when she called me closer
asked me to bring her crow painting
to stay straight across from her feet
so she could waken into it,
          remember her friend.

Of Old Chief alongside her shoulder
                still watching over her
just as the mountain had done
throughout her Alberta childhood.

The Pendleton shroud bearing our braids,
her figure in flaming pyre.

The cards, the notes, the tasks
the things undone,   not done
and she with us   faraway
as this has always been   and ever
will continue.

We meet we leave
we meld and vaporize from whatever
it was that held us human

in this life.

And all the beautiful things
that lead our thoughts and give us reason
remain despite the leaving and
all I know   is what you know

when it is over said and done
it was a time
            and there was never enough of it.

— I —

NAVIGATION

for life

STREAMING
for Sherwin & Travis

Ya,yan,e,tih
kettle
Yah,re,sah   Ya,yan,quagh,ke
beans, cornfield
Yat,o,regh,shas,ta
I am hungry

Once, we walk long grass into weave
pacing stem wrappings
in concentric circling;
southwise sans temporal sway,
beat to counts, not ticks
in a dream where time poses as dust,
where echo-wrinkles reverberate
consciousness signals against
savannahs—

Sandhills overhead, their chortling
carries snow geese back to councils.
In this streaming, seasons shift
far past distressed unravelings,
where grasses seed sparseness
commingle alongside wrinkle weavings, time,
signaling light shocks spreading fingerlike
across blue/white world—

Grass warp, weave, entwined, danced,
making mattress, woven mat
step crossing step, push/push,
making sure this place
brings matted dreamtime under
Dog Road, Darkening Land,
Cygnus, Swan, Northern Cross
echoing light/dark Albireo dreaming.

    Albeit night is with or without sun.

Circles align whether trampling
long stem beds over cracked earth,
into baited sun-whirled worlds,
whether north/cold, with or without light,
needling shafts through coarse indigos,
like velveteen, corded skeins, geese, yarn—

Somewhere woven; north of quipu hemp,
hemp laid moundwork blueprint, twined some
where north of periodical cicadas, mock locusts
now shivering night free with streaming song.

    Where light brings split shell husk, dry fly

appearances   under loosed locust ravished
leaf, 'neath not New Forest, but sweating
three-year Apache cicada who daylight
cannot swelter, no, cannot swelter nor
swing out across summer, cast into
swarming grasshoppers, winged, leaping

'neath cicada droning lovesongs, daylight
unimpeded desert caught in bleak receded
motion, overlapping, each trio member
keeping transparent winged vigilance.

Another cicada, here, north, now
prefers nightly monophony,
meatier female brings dreaming
tween utensil sticks we draw to tongue,
her veined wings set aside, soft burst
oral tradition, nourishment, medicine.

Three, thirteen, seventeen annuals
canopy contralto over unknown biomes,
under night waiting to break day
swallow it whole, lid shut, Leonids
rain over the closure, repeat passages,
stream, portal skipping, vortex threading,
weaving textural, lingual suffix, to stem/blade.

Some of us flew them, cicadas/Leonids,
    riding backbump, flying—

Some of us squirmed underworld with larvae, slick
retracing lives, Moon-Eyed passers, cavern travelers.

Some of us strictly scored trees,
edging along bark stream.
Some of us called night/day
for union after splitting
our backs open, crawling out into light, flying—

But now it's winter,
first fire forms stone mouths,
whispers, *go in there we're with you*
alongside, trio here, trio women.

Wherein, the waking gives acumen
already over, somewhere
further along stream east/south,
perpetual echo-wrinkling,
cicada songlike field wave
light/dark wrinkle, weave, here
corded skirts, woven petticoats
'neath mulberry bark skirts—

Sending us back where women
stood spearing, yellow poplar canoes
mooring, mooring cold water,
moving upstream when hot houses
gave them up, hoisted,
sent them above ground,
back to waters, thirsty, hungry.

Waterskipping spider spinning
fire/firing clay, clay painted
on poplar trunks, fired,
top to bottom, released to sail waters.
Released to sail, placed in tutsi bowl,
slung upon her back,
lightning fired, sycamore clothed,
fire, furnishings for home:

hot cicada, yellow jacket soup,
　　　　strawberry jam/nectar.

Here, in the cylindrical and spherical,
in the curvilinear space
its echo-wrinkle reverberations,
discernments, definitive dissonance;
here, intuition/memory intersect,
prophesy source into beingness,
we in certain presence—being—at all times.

On a river of variable stream, channel flow,
confluence, departures give wellsprings,
condition broad throughways,
water comes, proper placement,
nourishes life, causes sustenance. Come fruition,

informed by being, by elemental colliding
intersections within these planes,
within swell of source throughout elements, earth,
animal, plant: animate, inanimate.
Swelling echoes moving in seven directions,
spherical in a sense of reverb actions and response

in waves of knowns we perceive, collide into,
multidimensional, the sense of time, space, place—
the experiential impressed by a familiar spiritual sense.

A girl eyes next turn,
　　　　　　　gives melody to droning.

Caught her lostness with hemp skirt,
traveled down mountain,
Bluest Ridge, like fire from leaf to root,

like ice now mooring 'neath glacial melt,
now impending, lest we continue
along this way, newly invoked,
along this burn, stream, somewhere
between hummingbird/sloth,
between here/now, when/then,
vibration strum fissure,
variable stream, channel flow—

until we all come tumbling, find melody, until
we drone nightly, thrum—

Impressions strummed   today
incite future impulsion,
            create past prophecy.
Get it?

Along an echo-wrinkle in existence
    your presence permeates swaying.

Cries:

        Ya,yan,e,tih
            kettle
Yah,re,sah Ya,yan,quagh,ke
        beans, cornfield
    Yat,o,regh,shas,ta

I am hungry

Ya,yan,e,tih
kettle
Yah,re,sah Ya,yan,quagh,ke
beans, cornfield
Yat,o,regh,shas,ta
I am hungry

Ya,yan,e,tih
kettle
Yah,re,sah Ya,yan,quagh,ke
beans, cornfield
Yat,o,regh,shas,ta
I am hungry

Swaying permeates presence, your
    existence, in echo-wrinkle, along an
entry, chickadee messenger, cheeping
        this way, don't turn back.

Sloth carries hummingbird
alongside perpetual echo-wrinkling,
cicada songlike field wave
light/dark wrinkle, weave, here
corded skirts, woven petticoats
'neath mulberry bark skirts—

Clacking turtle hulls
shake world back into sequence.

Southwise turning
magnetic field migration.

Hummingbird fathoms navigation
along lekking glasswing routes,
sometimes monarchs, edge on milkweed
munch down Mississippi Valley
daisy fleabane, hackberry, willow.
                              Like silkworms
ceiling coved, mulberry leaved, cocooned
then boiled away to entrap threadpoint, unravel,
ravel, spin, wind, capture beauty in cloth

woven way east, here cotton carries life,
its weevils ever after emanating loss,
now monarch opens case, cleaves, light
enters day, moving waters, streams
from pit to wingtip, extending—shaking.

Cicadas droning, girl singing,
magnetic reason   cranes
float thermals, far past reason,
high in orbit break away in eight points,
approach in fours, return, approach,
like horse dance, for innocence, mares there
airbound approach, approach, dance
in channels, pathways, roads,

far below moonlight shimmers
sends locust tree her dressings.

Wear them, Sister, now your beauty
petticoats, mulberry—open-backed cicada—

Some of us flew them, cicadas/Leonids,
        riding backbump, flying—

Once, we walk long grass into weave
pacing stem wrappings
in concentric circling
southwise sans temporal sway,
beat to counts, not ticks
in a dream where time poses as dust,
where echo-wrinkles reverberate
consciousness signals against—

a dream echoing light/dark, some of us flew them.
        Albireo dreaming—   streaming.

        Ya,yan,e,tih
            kettle
Yah,re,sah Ya,yan,quagh,ke
        beans, cornfield
        Yat,o,regh,shas,ta
        I am hungry

        Ya,yan,e,tih
Yah,re,sah Ya,yan,quagh,ke
        Yat,o,regh,shas,ta

Ya,yan,e,tih
Yah,re,sah Ya,yan,quagh,ke
Yat,o,regh,shas,ta

I am hungry

Ya,yan,e,tih
kettle
Yah,re,sah Ya,yan,quagh,ke
beans, cornfield
Yat,o,regh,shas,ta

I am hungry

DRUNK BUTTERFLIES

Butterflies inebriated, sloshed
spiraling upward from pools of water
holding fermented foliage   we
passed by while canoeing the Neuse.
Orange, white, yellow, blue, black, brown
speckled, swallow-tailed, patterned,
mottled, webbed flash and quiver,
fluttering fine, fly, pit painted lady mating ritual.
Wrapping shyness with wing, undercover, under
folding blanket over lover.
Liquid courage emboldens beginnings, above
happenstance provision, easy prey for
prowling bird, turtle, fish, crawdad, frog.
The beauty of it all
in sunlightened wing shining, falling   forward and
back, up and down. Frenzy fantastic
color gentle, feathered wing too delicate to touch
without removing glide barb. Metamorphosed
just for this day
a metaphor, relational,
for all that is good and will be.
Butterfly girl wraps her hair into braided wing
flaps for future. Turns herself
into the softest touch, lifting and rising
everything around her, all that is good—
this is good—
something they do so much
better than the Human Beings

in natural accordance with traditional way
of the butterfly creation racing,
occurring in this way, for her and those following her.
Kama, kamama. Catch her
in the morning and
again at night, at midday she just floats by breezing.

EDDY LINES
for JTS

In transgressions
migrating song to stone,
au courant   your flint sparks
question each turn
waving over azimuth.

Brother, allow me to backpaddle, offer
bearing,   boil,   berry break—brace—
least we broach c-2.

In the chine,
a quail covey
awaits release,
as passenger pigeon
and Carolina parakeet
long over yaw
from foreigner squall—

Sternpaddler, you
call for reason
when sometimes
water just is and
the path we bear upon it
simply running
rock garden,   reading water,
quartering or purchasing
avoiding pitch, pivot, portage
for the freedom here.

Beyond the lob tree
a mouth opens.
We both go there

one after another.
First you, me.
Then me, you.
Our dugouts surely
best what lapstrake we make
sur le voyage.

Smoker ahead,
this yoke may come handy
despite shuttle duty.

One day
Kevlar may be essential
to offset keening.
For now, it's the cut of water,
the lean and what emboldens
each of us, singularly,
in the gradient.

I'll feather, you ferry,
until eddy lines
cross apart
and yet together
through this art—
          dead reckoning.

Perhaps, one day,
mapping courses
for one another,   lest
we forgive odds,
make mutual course,
loose branches so
some might follow
more easily.

WAITING FOR LIGHT
for Ted

Click click click on maple plank—
says she's seen some sense of light—
this rise, we'll move like prairie wolves toward
whatever's open, whatever receives poor
attempts at living, mutt and me, we'll be
quicker than the clicker she should be
trained with, now nestled in pockets,
in coats not come in time, not
ready for cold. Still a sense of here
is where we wring fear from fellows
born to page, pealing peel now pulp,
once slash-sewn fodder, click-tickling ivories
atop some far forgotten upright,
across a keyboard floor we move to.
Is it the last of us? What leads us
past the last window where
each of us finds light, dust? Whether it's coal
on cars, the 4:11, or voices sometimes pressed
to make the curve, make the State shine.
Shine on they say, and in this near light
embodying morning.
Coal heads east on the 4:11
sounding through sleepy streets
rumbling brick pavement, glass panes.
Time for tea, or coffee,
maybe Sumatran, or rooibos,
something imported, stamped.

Tornado-like whirring winds up, down rails,
velocity unknown, little matter,
inside this wood-floored, plaster-walled room.
Where the dog and I lie
waiting for sunrise,
waiting for light.

PLATTE MARES

Sandhill cranes rise into spiraled kettles, their
mares purring chortling kettling
                                        vortex siege
                                                    sedge herd.

Vortexing themselves into dawn, dusk.

Call & response.
Call & response. Call & response.
                                        Call   & response.

Tens of thousands looping high over mustang running buffalo sod.
Mares above, below.

Last year's colts breaking out into adolescent gangs, in
both worlds,   adolescent gangs, colt crane cohorts,
bachelor flock
              over colt mustangs turning.

The mares above turning yaw.

My filly snapping teeth on cool air.
Her lead mare calling, she neighs quick, call & response.

Sandhills display, spread wings, preen, arch, calling, fluff out
toward intruders   cranes, coyotes.
Mustangs pummel earth.

All mares facing off the canine bite.

Territory three to two-fifty acres—danced.

Nares, mandible,
          unison call, antiphonal territorial call, mated postures vocalized.

Over covert lining flight feathers,   primaries along the wing hand, propulse
forward,   secondaries,   forearm inside primaries, soar and stop,   tertials
of upper arm,   bustling close to the body—
estrous cycle   cloaca   oviduct—

Preparing for two egg clutch,
egg tooth tubercle horn. Precocial pipping breath,
hock tarsus—   The ground mares fetlock proofed as well, cradling foal.

Kettling, converging.

It is the season.

TED'S CRANES
for Kooser

Parachute glide down to Platte cool.
Must be a half million of 'em
landed last night. All I can see
is the poem Ted wrote when hard
freeze paralyzed them there, ice
hardened round their long legs
fastened death impending 'til shots
took life and fire carcasses. Here,
evening was gentle this time. Incoming
let down into flow with a bit of morrow
probable.

PHILOSOPHY

Last night,
I dreamed a small bird migratory rush
into a brushline nearby.

One of indiscriminate color, broke cover,
flew fast past the siege, directly into my open hand.

The bird stayed with me throughout my dreaming,
never left my palm
though it changed itself several times within my light clutch.

Was it bright?
It was bright.

SUMMER FRUIT

Plums hanging low.
Summer rain in reggae balm
below heat, here in
banana cherry slide—just right.
Just right.
Listen she's telling now:

Innocent—plum.
Succulent—plum.
Resonant—plum!
Swing plum
like yo-yo rum
like yo-yo rum
like yo-yo rum,
plum over, round,
into palm—plum.
Make it raspy—plum!

Firm flesh gives way
for finger, thumb
touch teasing easing plum juice
from
tantalizing fruit
spills
plum song
plum love
plum sweet touch
to whoever takes some

while
        summer has its way with us
                —'tis true.

Both of us
singing raspy plum juice
black cherry throat song
shadowed
in dark,
where duendes play
easy
lift light from
creases
opening flutter.

Is summer a box of light?
Box of fruit, opening?
Light streaming in all directions
fanning heat in rays spread,
sunshine through sheltering shade,
shadow dark embracing

offering light in each give, each
bend, every pressing hold
sheltering in radiance, resplendent.

Look here, sunshine in rain—brilliance—
like languages held in secret,
traditional tongues kept present,
nurtured, sheltered, in shade/sun,
light/dark, reed/oboe.

Her story, song—love
cradled in every
bit of wild planted sweet,
how she grew you, fills you now.

I remember the taste—love
remember him bringing promises, wine
playing his reed, oboe on cotton sheet
spread in summer swelter.
Island mountain sky,
box of light/shade
plum love
plum sweet touch
take some—

— II —

BREAKING COVER

for my sons

HEROES

   just go where they're made to
when everything else goes awry.

Eagle Tail in stilled time
the body lifting surface

where churning falls gave
walleye, trout, coolness
for multitudes, generations,

now quiver his resolute effort to
something larger than humanness.
                                 Was it?

Or, was it the core of humanness?
Was it melody? Rhythmic water
moving serpentine as it had always
grasped? Carrying, then delivering
the boy back to surface.

                       In turn taking in
the child's sister with brave stranger to
people the underneath where
we seldom belong.
                   Are they now nearer
the center we stepped from?

Nearer where we all lived,
yet gone? In this world we lose
the ones who give the most.

The fruit of toil, its mission.
More than we muster.

                Each time the water
surges and crashes, I feel his words,
I got him. Hold on to me. I won't let go.

PANDO/PANDO

The Trembling Giant Aspen / Bolivian massacre site

Trembling giant
   bulging under siege
Pando
  /Pando

waving I spread
   banned from streets
perpendicular to leaf blade
Pando/
   Pando

   havoc, natural gas
petiole flattened
   opposition pushing right autonomy
rush, lift, breaking cover, tremble
   on the fourth day of
yellow-white-grayish-yellow
Pando/Pando

   hunger strike, assailants
   lobbed a green grenade
   forced to knees   shirtless
   peasantry
tree
Pando
  /Pando

Pando/
    Pando
aspen man spreads uprising
flowering, flower,
spreading root sprout
Pando
    ambush
    where Morales has stayed
biomass   clone cross   giant uprising
deeply rooted Indigenous growth
    prevent Bolivia from splintering apart
Pando/Pando

    visiting Santa Cruz
one hundred acres
    dynamite blasts
fourteen million pounds
    public humiliation
Pando/Pando

rooted eighty thousand years
    fifty Indigenous mayors rooted
    thirty Andeans killed this week
    paralyzed borders
    Argentina, Brazil, Paraguay
Pando/Pando
clonal colony
    colonial massacre
singular genetic individual
    Morales, an Aymara Indian,
Pando/Pando

organized opposition, university
student conservatives, forced terrified
Indigenous people, to their knees
forced refugee people to
apologize for coming to Sucre
forced chanted insults to their hero Evo
then conservatives set fire
to blue, black, white Aymara flag
seized hand-woven Aymara ponchos
Aymara people
Pando/Pando

Pando/Pando
rhizome, basal shoot
    shot,   seven dead
shooting—genet/ramet
    peasant farmers

organism overtaking
    not supported by current evidence

Fishlake quaking
    Amazon
    Pando
aspen   life in largest
    singular germination
Pando/Pando
    Pando/Pando
Pando/Pando
    Pando/Pando
Pando/Pando

Pando/Pando
Pando/Pando

SWARMING

Swarming upward
hosts thicken air as hornets
with whirling winds
their weapons wielded wildly

back home blackbirds whirl
in skies grayed
from icy winter chill, frost,
a single sparrow cowers against
bush base huddling

wind bristles with his war
skies hustle
fields, valleys, meadows moan
mountains reel

all creatures
cater to whims of man
in chaotic frenzy for battle
when peace is ever present
in just one thoughtful breath

breathe, breathe deep

HIBAKUSHA

Each breath depends upon life
easing lungs: child & elder.
Every inkling, cause for peace.

Each moment offering time,
simple presence with still hands
streaming over darkened light.

Sharing inhale, exhale, peace—
Calling, *come to this.*

STEEL

Boerum Hill, Little Caughnawaga
where the glamour boys of structural steel sleep

Skyline depended on them one hundred
twenty years, six generations. Mohawk
crews fashioned the city, iron dressed
and floated her into ether.

                              After the fall,
everyone, clear to Zuni, put on call, smoke-
jumpers, seventy, eighty percent Native
crews, lived it, in the heat: colonization,
construction, that morning, this day,
every beam in balance despite horror
in the world.

STORY

So my sister,
works down near Water,
got off her printing shift 'bout
time things all came down.

All the hustle, she thought
a bus wreck. Kept going,
ahead, out of their way, eyes
down,   *way to make it in the city, right?*

By the time she got a call out
to me, they were looking for her
from work, wondering if she'd
made it off the subway before
the whole thing buckled.

Few days on, she was wiping
windowsill dust, when light
dawned on her, was ash, remains
cremains, probably. Huddled there
after flying out of towers, now blown.

SEARCHING GROUND

Every bit of them apart,

like my sister's cat when
she hit twenty, a claw or two

remaining behind when she
stepped off army blankets
from wwii, into 2001—

everything in pieces.

1973

Things come full circle, back to where they started.
That's Revolution. —RUSSELL MEANS

It was war by any fine-toothed measure.
When hunkered down in Grandma's belly
culled prickling quill resistance shuddered
bunkers filled with fifteen-year-old horsemen
shielding her tongue like any warrior would.
When it was over, the tanks and troops shivered
their way back to doom. Manifest licked wounds.

leciya o iyokipi

SOLAR FLARES

solar flare
noun Astronomy
a brief eruption of intense high-energy radiation from the sun's
surface, associated with sunspots and causing electromagnetic
disturbances on the earth, as with radio frequency

communications and transmissions—

At work, everyone smiling bellicose
through teeth staked together
jutted over clenched knees
all knotted there.

The Platte poured over choked
in ice jams,   floated past
blocking all exits west.
Droid compass
stroked message spelled:
Atypical Electromagnetic Field Detected.

My finger near my ear
gestured south, so still,
turning was the only way out.

Somewhere in this,
I posted:

Wisconsin Aid:

To supply protesters with WATER *contact*
Capitol Center Foods at 608-255-2616.
To supply protesters with FOOD *contact*
Burrito Drive at 608-260-8586,
Silver Mine Subs at 608-286-1000,
Ian's Pizza at 608-257-9248,
Pizza Di Roma at 608-268-0900,
or Asian Kitchen at 608-255-0571

on the union listserve.
Seniority tuned-up
lodging complaint
"misuse of internet"

knees, mandibles clacking—

Me, I watched
Which Way Home
dreamed more for the children there
and isn't that why we organized, anyway? This flaring?

FIRST MORNING
for Nancy

DC STR #1 Adams House Suite

In a room facing chimneys
over the place Nancy Morejón rests
between sleeps lining free lines
she whispers to hearing DC:
Obsidiana, Vilma en Junio,
Un Gato Pequeño A Mi Puerta.

Morning is birdsong
in an old Spanish town.

Though the chief
in his acquired misery
echoes Kenya until he breathes
life into malady, or at least compels
us so to believe, she sleeps with
Africa, Canton, and other points slavery
turn Cuban in her bone breath
bringing love, embrace, freedom from
whatever holds the rest of us in weight.

The lifting is simple, yet
without it how sad we all be.

Embargo=fear
Yet here she is!

Sugaring our boughs before we break.

BARRIO TRICENTENARIO,
PLAZA DE BANDERAS

Wading footsteps of murdered
in the barrio Juan calls home
we sing our songs, tell stories,
cry a bit when conquistador
reenactors dance in color.

Botero blasted away refilled
with forty sculpted doves,
in the city where from here
I love you deeply and from
there it was but a night.

Butterflies fill streets
verse winging ways fluttered
by faces middling dark hours
leveling light.

        Here you held
my hand, urged I follow, let
Bogotá beckon while we
played our voices for victims
recalled by lovers, grandmas,
niños still swimming Escobar wakes.

NIÑO DE LA CALLE

A few coins?   Can I leave you?
Can I walk by without leaning in
holding you close, telling you
stars' pathway beyond this math?

Niño de la calle, every evening
moving from the huffing voom
to isolated despair, translucent,
like me once,   and I love you, I do.

They tell me nothing can be done,
the boys, gone to glue, abandoned here,
believed gone. And I know the boy who
left lockup for reservation home who
returned to us his mind half-gone, so
the asylum brain scan shown. I know.

Yet, here, your eyes, damn it—
Can I not leave this duty, the state, reach
down, lift you, remember my own soul
starved, muffled, what then?

Each boy our son.

CAMPOS

In the camp, children
suckle popsicles, ice cubes,
turn tops same as every era

sprawling north picking
someone else's money,
handing it over in leathery
balls, in tiny hearts, in stiff
shoots they cradle, held there

reverent to tastes, savory,
clutched, cradled, caressed
for someone else's table.

DUBLIN CROSSING
for Jill

Gulls call over black pool morning
            stout night,   still sleeps.

The Blue Boy, The Magdalene Laundries,
everything echoes   past, passed
across waters   black robed,   anointed
colonial crime.

Two days ago, on Pearce, past Trinity
a young man on his stoop, adjusted himself
to my eyes, then vanished. The door was 146.

Tricks the dead give when we move with them.

In life, we bridge rivers, charge ha'penny crossings,
trade things, abandon—

In the end, each child crucified splits scenes, bides.

WAS MORNING CALL
for Ibrahim & LeAnne

It was morning call streaming some emic encoding, ceremonial invitation, invocation mood-altering song, stilling wanderlust premise into meditative contemplation, into internalized presence, familiar. After the first dawn, we awaited every other, from hotel rooftops or friends' balconies, juxtaposed there against sky and sound in shared sense no matter the difference. There is none, in that place. If you are in. We came to it. My son and I scan the edges of courtyards, alleyways, between building spaces for cats looking something like we haven't seen in cats before. Something specifically natured Amman, or anywhere else cityscaped we happened to move toward. It was figs, olives generously let into our armholds by Basma smiling or any number of wonderful soulful women who were so happy to meet us, thrilled we attempted language, fond with memories of attending schools in North America, back not long ago. It was whistles for children, clicks for calls, weddings every night in the lobby and ballroom, music, music, music, and song. It was Sufi chanting away angers and misunderstandings when other people from our countries grieved them with inconsiderate proselytizings, demands, or senseless banter. It was feeling funny when called a sa-vage and responding that's what they try to tell us about you, too, shared laughter echoing back, o Indi Ahmed. Art stunning apartment walls around Ibrahim Nasrallah and more writers' union poets. Wine, Palestinian, opened just for us after being bottled for so many decades discussion ensued to recall the variables. It was humus for pennies, oil so soft, the scent of it, fragrant, endearing. It was qahweh for free and chayi for almost nothing. Bits of fruit and desserts given as samples simply to celebrate someone attempting to order in Arabi, like me. It was cab rides through asthma for fifty cents when others were charged so ridiculously we all gathered round to laugh at the foolishness. Camels and Bedouin camped on the road just outside town. Bedouin, calling us Bedouin, too. King's crows, hooded, black, white, black, hang around King Abdullah's grave, longing for royal handouts, tourists tolls, guilt debts, manners of monarchy. It was morning call streaming some emic encoding, invocation, mood altering, stilling brought us home in some shared known never faltering despite the bullets streaming, in spite of ourselves. Stilling for a song, singing.

HATCHLINGS
for LeAnne

Here we hatch like robin eggs   split shells
lying near tree talking base,   creaking,
clearly knocking   out loud through ovaled trunk
into split shoulder blades   as you stand singing aside her.

She a mother tree, matriarch like you, Anitsata,
hosting half-dozen daughter-sisters surrounding her.
You with your Southern head above grass, leaves, waters,
under skies ripe with Wampano/Quiripi in a place
skated in poet-wielded canoes, some standing balanced, rowing.
    We both know—

Here,   *l, n, r, y*   dialectical embrace
asunder   *a, b, c—z*   notions child's play.
Nothing near Mercy Nonsuch, nothing
Nehantic left to this Old Lyme section, or is it?

We muse lingua franca,   1658 catechism, pidginized—
rudimentary ruse relishing   our retreat to this river shore,
where, here, we note loss,   burning undergrowth forgotten
steering deer ticks toward their painful human pleasures.

In this place known for speaking grounds, knocking things—
This place of Borrelia burgdorferi, mimicking Euro-gifted
syphilis,   from white-footed mice, sure-footed deer—
Like Little Deer who punished with rheumatism touch, back
    where we're from.
    For those who had no reason—

Here we are hatched into this place ripened with paper splitting
   shell language
loss lingering long, limbs lifting hatchlings into lingual-tongued
   blue shell shaken skies.

PEANUT POND

Under poplars, maples
between turtles, black bass,
beauty between   pollen
skimmed   waters,
Canadians,   two pair,   lead
at least twenty-four goslings,
creep in from human worry
nearer peeper lives.
Heron swoop dailies,
kerosene-lighted nights.
Sometimes duty fails academic.
Poetry, practice of everything else:
paddled waters, lilies, samaras,
pine needled, caned sprigs,
some sweet vine
wraps hollow maple
flowering while I pen
over your writing
in the base of this canoe.
Mooring for a moment
over waterworlds below.
Only shift,   paddle dip.
To still, straighten.

CARCASS
for Ceca

Carcass kindled like a rucksack
jerky-filled snack for Crow & Beetle.
Split skin stretched over marrowless cage,
encased dry tomb, like those strewn
through this loess reach, cradling past
ever present here, and now you come
walking riverside, bringing sensory thrill
into daylight much like this Cervidae
culled morning each waking before
demise. We move this way, catching life
until death captures us, where we rot
into the same dust holding multitudes
before us, and welcoming those beyond.
We lift this measure. Toss casing, frame to
wind over shoulders, swaddling human
in ruminant mammal rim, softening intake
in sleek steps alongside rivered bellies
like stones turn time back into brink.

Here, where I find you dovetailing wind
into hoofprint, your antler turned away
as if to sway yourself back. Me, I follow,
wrapping myself, enclosed interment, where
we peek from time to time, huddling here,
heaving morning, lifting once more, dense
fog from repository remains we quicken
in paint, punch key pummel. 'Tis the nest

of this that brings us here. 'Tis the hide
we wallow. Carcass veil blanketing morning
like this foot feels split hooves, now
knuckled deep between us two. He's
with us all the way to page, leading,
death propelling promise, revisit, renew,
rekindle—'Tis the seat of it now. 'Tis the life—
River come clean carcass, makeover mad
rush with insight, first dawn taste—take.

MAY SUITE

WEATHERBAND/FM/AM
2013, Moore, Oklahoma

After a while you can't hear about it anymore,
switch to something more melodic
shift to something Heart & Soul
92.1/1140 KRMP
Cowboys of Color Rodeo
soothes you   wind blown
when the Teacher of the Month comes
grade school disciples shield
fixurlifeup, fix your life up.

WE WERE IN A WORLD

We were in a world, in a world, in a world. Sure, we had our glyphs, but we were providential. Once, some alphabet believers, glass purveyors, Ursus Arctos killers, sent all bailiwick on cursed course far faster gyration backspin, birling intrinsic angular momentum—boson melts. Spinning, it careened away iceberg, iceberg, iceberg; glacier braced time traced yesterday unshakable base—all below flushed alluvion torrent, Niagara pour, special spate, flux, flow, until their coastal citadels moldered from cyclone, tsunami, hurricane gale. Tornadoes tossed turf wherever they pleased. Eruptions molded Her back into something She deemed worthy. *Not to mention quakes.* And the people, the people, the People, pushed into cataclysm, a few generations from alphabet book imposed catechism, soon were calamity tragedy storm splinters, fragmented particles of real past, in a world gone away from oratory, song, oraliteratures, orations into gyrations reeling. Soon hot, hot, hot, hot, hot, hot, hot, hot, hot. Hot, dying mangroves, disappearing Waimea Bay, dengue fever, butterfly range shift, meadow gone forest, desert sprung savanna, caribou, black guillemots, bats, frogs, snails—gone. *What will sandhill cranes crave?* Winged lay early. Reefs bleach. Rain, rain, rain, rain, rain, rain, rain, snow, snow, snow, fires flaming fiercely, fascinated in their own reflecting glare. Marmots rise early. Mosquitoes endure longer, lasting biting spreading West Nile. Polar bears quit bearing. Robins, swallows, enter Inuit life. Thunder finds Iñupiat. Here, it is said, glyphs left rock wall, stone plates, bark, branch, leapt animated into being, shook shoulders, straightened story, lifted world upon their wing bone, soared into Night, to place World back into socket eased sky—stilled us. Some say the soup leftover was worded with decolonized language. Some say the taste lingers even now.

IN THE YEAR 513 PC

In the year 513 PC—post-contact, post-Columbus, post–cultural invasion—In the year, 513 PC, we heard fluting sounds from southern feathered, feathered never here before this rhyme, never here without zookeeper logic trace. Never. No. Prior to this vast erasure those sounds fell way below equator, left us here without the slightest notion all along. Now robins sing early, leaving them hungry for later worms. Now no bird's leaving, tides receding, waters capture sand like evening fog: Virgin Islands, Galápagos Islands, Cook Islands, Belize Barrier Reef, Red Sea Reefs, Great Barrier Reef, Tokyo, Jakarta, London, New York, New Orleans— we've seen it quarter blown—engraved. Big Easy slipping far past fate of no return, her trumpets flaring. We're all a jazz funeral display, singing, dancing, masking ourselves to crypt enclave. Banging drums, sounding horns, driving ourselves while making faces leap from costumed weathermen; back to wards, social clubs, quarters. Not so surprising in a place where nothing counts, unless it's Creole singing. Looking back, signs gave taste to trepidation, foretold all ten years to known. If we'd only seen the writing, bird tracks left etched on earthen wall. 513 you'd scarcely remember until it had all been drowned. Someone still calling, "Saving the Earth is not a competition, but an essential collaboration."

TWISTIN' THE NIGHT AWAY
2013, Oklahoma

How that man in evening clothes got here
well, you know,   feel much better.
Sometimes dancing's all we got.
Sometimes move with it,   we rock.
Sometimes take off, see him   go,
just like any other show,
when that wind comes
oldest queen
don't you know just where we'll be
down with Red Dirt, Deep Deuce way
feel much better.

                       Twistin' twistin' twistin' the night away.

— III —

WHERE WE HAVE BEEN

for my father

TAXONOMY

Mornings made delirious, scrambling into thread
out from dreaming, wrangling ways past delusion
into streets unpaved, unproven, unmet. It was hard-
over, no sunnyside—easy—and the only yolk—seated sky—
rose streaming over the lot of us quickened in some
strain no corona could bear resting, lean. Then
the mesa sat standing wayside, case some giants made
their way back into meantime, met us here, met us.

We were tabooed, shunned, mocked and on our mettle
most any pierce of day. Principal struck blows to show we
deserved no mercy. It was splintering. Holes bored blisters
each smacking wave. We were deserving. Wave after wave
first grade took the test out from me. Never did spill again,
no matter the syndrome. We were anything but beggars,
so we scraped by, held up. We flung ourselves into every
angle, withheld our curve. Split loose from whatever held on.

Motown made our mercy. Only soothe in western rooms
rounded in radio waves gleaning out the insides of maternal
mind. Unkind charge firing synapse beyond reasoning goals.
She moved through it like lightning, charging each wave
with serious challenge, but nothing made it bearable and
hands down was just a game call brag. Only hands down we
laid was on ball courts. Home front was daily challenge, there
was nothing certain other than each day just like the last.

Lest they moved you, sent you off to foster somewhere no
one warned might reckon. Sent you streaming. Gave you up

like paper. Tossed, crumpled, straightened up, and smoothed out flat. That was that. It was nothing you'd remember, but we do. Still taste that strangeness surrounding ones who go between, move through other worlds while in this one. No one lives like we do, least it seems so, always on the mind. Why? Never time to question and still don't know. Only thing we know we are different and not like you and even though we try three times harder it never works out right. No, nothing takes the sting of it, or scent either. We look off, sound off, give off a presence everyone else knows stay away and they do, so far from us we walk sideways vanishing points return to horizons soaking us in, distinguishing us. Mettle in our mouths as well, steely, and steal we did, still do, no one's got more lift than us, no one's got more hunger. How about the time they made us breakfast, real one, over that pancake house off of 40, remember? Dad's Christmas to us right before seeing her in The Pavilion, little dish of butter looks like ice cream to kids like us. Made the eggs slide over easy just like he did before the madness. *Man this is rough country, get that straight. Mettle this!*

SUDDEN WHERE

Talon-plucked speckled trout from bitterroot bed, splish
dream through cloud swells, turbulence imagining comfort
on the way to forever. It's the shake of it, the sudden where, like
tossing suitcases into corners lent for foster kids untangling
claws still extended. Not the best of us, no, not near what we
once were, still only children, we scraped by, skinning knees
on borrowed bikes, traded at the B & D. Cousin tamed since
no one else had time to tender. Was a working world, cast
out toothbrush hanging wherever a hook held still enough.

Nine lives by nine, cut, torn, blasted to bits all around us.
Walls sometimes plastered with brain noodle. In some
fascination-led Western, so & so. Was it our baseball coach
showed us conceal? Marched us in Sears & Roebuck, night
before her wedding, wanted something scanty little girls could
ease outside without losing dimes, much less dollars. No, coins
better spent at any skating drive-in joint. Teens hanging over
Mustang glass, blinking easy, leaving all intendeds, puffs,
smoke, bottled-down splash to sink secure, like fishing, like
something some winged friend would come down this way for.

She was good to us, even when we couldn't be to one another.
Save the lifting, her heft carried us through. Far more than Siebert
pranks, stealing plums when uncle carefully turned his head a-shy.
Only a baby then, that was way back. No, here we were nine, or so,
just old enough to flee the 'napper in filthy white pickup, come to
carry us home, his, maybe never come back, but we ran, yes, ran,
right round corners, alleyways, fields crossed the way to coach

who threw down, challenging the perv, 'til he fled from what he knew.
Next year they had me up in Leoti, riding killer horses, crow on
shoulders, toughened up like Clint might be, I was the High Plains
Drifter at ten. Least that town thought so. A Woodlands girl here emboldened.

Never right for roping. Just running all through time. Split some-
times, just to joke it. Before laughter was real. Back when hard was
a given, a gist for gimmicking while winding backroads with
the curved spine of kids who stayed hungry. What was food? Mac 'n' cheese,
plums when one could steal some, peanut butter stirred with a spoon, oily,
tasty. Now & then someone took us fishing. Maybe bluegill, maybe crappie,
maybe we'd find something magnificent, give it up to make somebody happy.
Far from us, anyways, we thought we were. Thought we were unbreakable,
tried so many times to snuff ourselves—each other—blunders were our closest
friends. Kept us from soaring over cloud dreams, swimming in deep water,
skimming surfaces in grasslands without a notion when we'd make it back
to the piney mountains calling us home. That was fostering. Sudden where.
Being left to airs, to talons lifting, sometimes tearing scales as they raised us.

STRIKING CHORDS

French braiding her hair for the first time,
my place in Cundiyo, up on Rio Santa Cruz,
so far into our thirties our favs were classic past,
we glimpsed into sistering like four-year-olds
wondering what else was lost to us, our world
augmented with pianist's blues.

Mom hammering peddles, ivories, hard
melodies punctuating some strange prelude.
Coffee and cigarettes, her basic falter
as she tickled peculiar parallels between
ceilings, curiosities, tumbled up-
side down with illogical clues.

Kept us held there, caught up in wonder
for something unreal, unseen, she knew.
When wanderlust set in, we left one another,
striking wide world, each alone, unproven tunes,
harbor melancholy underneath long
hair left loose to pull us through.
Now gathering chords,
                    arpeggio, we two.

MEASURING UP

It wasn't socks missing from his feet,
not elbow cloth unraveled unilaterally,
not equal displacement of chin and brow,
nor the eye that sat a bit lower on the right,
it was his knuckle that made me weep,
clove corners gone wayside, like miniscule meat
hooks clawed away bits of him each shift he made,
invisible a timeliness unfurled. It was his muscle
torn through, festering, the prosthetic hand, finger-
width dismay all across his attempted grin, left
there just like that, for anyone to see—it was his mercy.
In the end we're rarely beautiful, mostly placed
away from compromising situations into poses
offsetting what has become of us in some gawker's
unnerving eyes. Yet, he was, is, still here in mine,
and I'm human because of it. Maybe only. Maybe.

THEN

Black Blizzard—hundreds of thousands of years to create the topsoil. Red from Oklahoma, Texas gray, brown Nebraska. The animals sensed it coming before the people. Chickens went to the coop and stayed there. The animals ran unsensibly, unreasonably. Clouds of dust made human figures in the wind. Could be an hour, or minutes to arrive. People fastened wires to the house to follow back—you could be blown away. Visibility no more than a few feet. Massive dusters. Some for days—during school hours—ten years of this. Silt on everything. Families daily digging out. Every surface in the house coated. Dust in food before it could be eaten, still eaten, field dirt with the food. Covering windows and doors with cloth, sheets, paste—air thickened, dimmed. Cloth to face felt awful—suffocating—dust, pneumonia took children. Radiation dry heat transfer, Kansas mercury 121. Insects seeking moisture, shade, centipedes, had to shake out shoes, sheets. Swarms—grasshoppers, gophers, birds gone from the dust, nothing to eat them. Jackrabbits multiplying, badgers, coyotes gone. Ten thousand took part in a rabbit drive. Thirty-five thousand jacks caught in a pen. They clubbed them to kill them, men killing them, rabbits screaming, while static electricity, from friction, took lives, sparked everywhere. Plain sand charged metal, blue flames, ball lightning, same safety wires lined to find houses—cars charged up with static, knocked people out, livestock ran in circles, lungs filled with dust—dead—only water 100 feet below, Sears & Roebuck sold windmill kits to fix up. Dad, ten. People ate tumbleweeds, then.

AGAINST THE BARREL

It was here against the barn, against the barrel,   Dad, as a boy, tipped forward
    leaning into something double-cocked to split-ease his pain.

Sam upon him daily, riding ridicule, hanging wooden signs upon his shoulders:
        "Cheap Indian Labor For Sale."
He was not for sale.   This, at nine, he knew.

Here, he'd thought of his sister, Rose,   Rose, Sam had tried to trade
for a boot hook,   in the days when boot hooks were cheap, common.
Contemplating reason he might let go—
Here
        he considered the changeling,   Sam,   all the siblings certain he was
placed within their nest   as though a brother.   Here, against the barrel steel,
he
deliberated his fury, his grasp,   leaned
                                a little further into openness there, split shot
sequencing—

Luckily Lucy, his hero-sister, came around this corner,
cried to him, "Don't,   'cause I won't stop you, so they'll just blame me."

She knew his passion, knew his wrongings, knew decision—not.
Knew without her he would soon go right out of this world.

Instead, she sat with him while they pretended not to cry.
Stilled him.

So we could pass here knowing, right here in this dust, she delivered him to us.
So we could pass here thinking of our father,   his boyhood shame.
So we could pass here—

pass—here—against every Sam Scratch—

Pick up the long barrel,   lean in,   put it back down.

DUST: DAD'S DAYS

Dust storms darkened sky so, you couldn't
find your way around house, yard.
Crack thick as a postage stamp gave way
to dirt through walls,   to black blizzard.

Dirt in food—in everything.

Damn it, the dust storms
three days at a time.
Couldn't see.

Dirt scratched, confused.
Some people lost their minds, killed their families.

Rabbits, grasshoppers everywhere, billions came.
Billions of grasshoppers at everything.

Rabbits,   hares, really.
Jackrabbits, had been in breaks by creeks.
Bad weather came, they moved to flats. Stressed
rabbits, hares, bearing six to eight young,
instead of two, three in litters.

Our fox terriers chased rabbits wildly.
The Border collies trained them to herd
them in, catch them.

Us Cherokee, all surrounded by Missouri Mormons.

Not as far out as Utah Mormons
who believed lizard language, angels.
We'd come out for the work there, freedom—
Cherokee hunkered there in the dust, missing mountain green.

Come winter, blizzard winds howled and
howled and howled and howled and howled.

Windmill was all you could make out in ground blizzards.
Everything whited out so bright, you'd think everything was nothing.

Windmill would freeze, have to heat it
with pans of hot water,   unseize it.
Cattle horses drink on one side,
Prince the Percheron stallion, on the other.
Only my brother Willis could hitch Prince and Doll.
She'd walk along, he'd pull.
Dolly, an older cattle mare, would discipline Prince.
He'd defer to her, even as an adult.
No matter his size.
She was his boss.
Dust was our boss.

Sweet corn, beans, pumpkin, squash, and tomatoes.
Six rows beans, six corn, switch
back and forth annually.
People used a Go-Devil to cut back what they called weeds.

Times were thrashing beans, snapping corn—
We stripped ears of corn, threw into wagons,
corn sheller gave cobs for winter fuel.

Dry cow chips for summer fuel.
Everything operated on one-boy-power:
laundry, cob fuel, chips—wagons full.

Made good crops till 1932. '33, the wind came, the dirt storms.
1934, gave it up, moved away,

That land should have never taken plowing
like the Whites around us gave it.
The drought killed us. Killed us. Killed us.

Shouldn't have happened.
They'd lifted the herd sod.
Took the drumhead off the topsoil.
Loosed it until it was crumble.
Reckless. Recklessness. Recklessness.
Dust.

Dad said. Before WWII,
before they found out it was more
efficient to fly one direction over another,
they didn't understand jet streams.

The *Sonoran high*
moved north, took it all.
Fall 1935-6-7-8 and on, threw a sack
around a shoulder, dragged behind,
picking left and right, we hit the cotton fields,
picking people's crops, any left.

Tallyman recorded how much.

Flies, sweat, back ached and ached
for a penny a pound—dust.
Teenager might pick a hundred
pounds in a day, make a dollar.
Older people more efficient,
maybe make two, three dollars a day.

We were always thankful for offers, *come pick,*
money so hard to come by.
Good owner'd say, "Why don't you
eat some watermelons?"
Angle his finger toward some melons
growing alongside the cotton,
raised for pickers' pleasure
to keep us half-fit.

Dust, insects, sweat, aching back, dust, dust…
Everything dust. Everything dust.

LEFTIES

Grandpa Herb's left elbow
took a Mauser bullet, World War I, traced
his brown forearm like a sleeve seam, red ridged track
'top skin showed when he pulled the fiddle down,
since plucked right instead of left, played
through egged mornings, Chinook dawns, pancaked right.

Scrambled, boiled, poached,
he'd crack any sort of egg you'd like.
Stood them alongside hotcakes—kept them coming,
kept them coming, so each morning break you'd rise
awakened with the scent of story,
every morning   in his mapled house.

E do di, Grandpa Vaughan, long before my time,
leaded graze Dust Bowl Depression haze when
something animal, once shown itself,
            miracle in time of not.
Deer, rabbit, bear—we've all forgotten.

His handgun thrown quickly over his right forearm,
for balance, braced, targeting down   take
to feed the family, feed their hunger,   feed them.

In an instant he moved, rote, familiar—
Iver Johnson 5 shot snub nose .38—
Something in the weariness wobbled
him to low aim, took bullet

into his own flesh, fumbling
like his boys on practice catgut strings.

Story goes, he came home, quiet.
Everyone wondering why his left arm
was wrapped, so large, what went on—
Finally, in frustration, he confessed his error,
not complaint, just information, then forever sleeved
another notch in the nothingness of the thirties.

From World War I to dust drug on,
my grandpas both distinguished
in the ways of wounds.

Each periled with sensibility of feeding the family.
Each prepared in moment of mire.
Each present in peril feeding us
in bullet-riddled stories surrounding
sweet fiddle feedings for our hearts.

WEALTH

When it was over

everything dust   blown
chickens, ducks, horses, plows
Model A, Mark III

   Dad still keeps the key
mounted to this tin shed wall.

Dust, then,
       everything blown.

Dust, dust, dust.

Still they came around
asking for whatever he held
       to feed,
eleven of them he carried
and the others,   dozens.

Grandpa the generous
gave his last rhyme
in riddle rhythms
without capital consensus.

"I thought you were rich."
They said.

As Granddad and his family
walked away from this
repossessed dugout,
chunk of ground,
earthen home,

flushed and empty,
chin up, Cherokee . . .

"Am, my family's alive."
He affirmed, shaking his head loose
from assumption
he had anything left to give.

As if he'd ever been fund wealthy
longer than a week.

Still Granny fed them
before they walked on.

He insisted. She couldn't imagine
                any other way.
It was their manner. Their spark.

Once, his land had put out,
he gave away 'cause others called,
split between closer relatives
who camped all alongside throughout.

Until it was done.

Back to corn, squash, beans, tomatoes.
Back to working for railroads,
farmers, farriers, friends, foes.

Back to the shoulder plow,
another hold, far from rooted homes,
rotted worlds behind them,
then the dust,

        dust,   dust,   dust.

Still, in this world,
down generations now.
Others come wanting
        something
                they're sure we have.

We pull out our checkbooks, cards,
overdraw ourselves.

Feed them.

KAOLIN

From dust comes dysentery;
comes dysentery cures
from clay.

White, red lingerings
linings for belly stops.

Kaolin, kaolin
light gray clay
softly soothing
all else matters.

From dust we may
to dust return, slip,
all the while soothing
itself—kaolin.

RAINMAKER

Daddy promised rain.
Each time he brought in turtles, always
conjured, stirred memories, brought help.

Said, somewhere in memory, wherein rain swells,
Se mu and Se lu ally, o he reh, nay hah,
Kichwa, Cherokee, Mohawk, Oendat still unite
through the Mother of the world—ourselves.

Somewhere in rain, World's woes relinquish, float downstream
in muddles, undercurrent, overflow, ebb, eddy, wash clean—
clay or tin gutters in red-yellow Sun.

Gutters spilling rain into buckets,
into trenches dug around our caliche yard,
like World War II, Dad's Ring of Fire
fieldwork,
    for the infantry,
      in rain.

Quenching his dry cotton memory,
Dust Bowl's crazymaking drought dread.
Rain was always there,
hovering high, waiting for soothing song
to heal sunbaked soil, eroding.

Somewhere in dreams clatter turtle shells
turning World back inside herself

Cherokee, Creek recall memory, memory, memory—
back into ourselves—
    raining.

Raining, here on Orinoco, here where moriche palm
hammock wrap Warao dreamtime, recollect Seminole
sleeping 'neath chickee, like palafito, stilted thatched
overhang where hammocks wing
night air over fluting crickets
loud as the amaranth, Caracas traffic,
maestoso as Florida amaranth still rising full.
    Still there is rain.

Every river—rain, every creek, burn,
swamp, delta, pond, ocean—rain.
Rain holds memory, dreamtime,
                        all that was, will be—
turtled under canopies
from Atlantic to Caribbean blues,
hulling all the loss, all the beauty, all that was:

    Carolina parakeets.
    Passenger pigeons.
    Venezuelan oily birds gone to conquistador war lights.
    Canaries, still suffering souls for coal.

Above, below,   rain returns realtime,   now here,
empathy, nourishment,   light,   life—

Causer, taker of winged, splayer, separator of souls, washout—
even rain can't help you.

But a human of the earth, place, time—memory—
takes a turtle—
Daddy called for rain
Daddy called for rain
Daddy called for rain
Daddy called for rain
Daddy called for rain
Daddy called for rain
Daddy called for rain
Daddy called for rain.
Like we all always do.
Always do.
Like we will always do.
Always do.

SHE SHAKES CHILIES FROM HER HAIR

She shakes red chilies from her hair,
wax black with slight red strands, thick enough
to stand, hold spicy seasoning until we fall.

Chilies she shakes loose, caught in leaning against red
ristas, hung loosely on rose adobe walls.
Summer we greet our spiciness from time before.

Shakes chilies she attracted, red as wasps,
something winging while she stands swinging
her heavy mane. Loosing it from flavor, season.

Spice in life rife with something only sisters share.
    Red chilies she shakes from her hair.

COTTON

Standing stooped, walking rows
quicker than those dropped to knees

crawling on dry ground, kneeling,
knee bone wearing earth,
earth wearing knee bone,
neither better for the wear
on those too big, or too weak to stand.

Stoop labor in cotton
carries more weight to field end.

Cotton cupped pricked bolls
require finesse, proper pick.

Oblige ordinary people
extraordinary extreme effort.

Grandpa Vaughan playing Pitch
with the farrier, his heart out long before
Dad was ten. Playing Pitch, cards
while Granny and their kids

picked the fields clean,
choked on dust, dusted themselves,

boll held green to split prongs
calling for clever

get in, pull out
without cutting fingertips wide open.

Walking on knees,
or walking bent

dust, insects, sweat
cotton, cotton, cotton

until the owner offered
watermelon at wind up

—if he was a good man.

INDIGO

Lost like last night's blues
leaning left, left—indigo.

Leavings, bits, pieces
scrap, twine
indigo.

Tally counts
penny shares.

Indigo.

Everyday

indigo, indigo, indigo.

Some shirttail cousin died,
all his pockets poked receipts
trade tobacco, cotton, indigo.

Blue slips
slipping through blue seam holes
fingered long blue in frustration,
fidgeting.

Slipping through the years,
like loss laces summer sky

indigo
indigo.

Indio.
In Dios.

Indigo.

TOBACCO RISE

Tobacco rises up 'neath Visqueen,
cool fog morning, coffee warmed

to wake where this field will take seedlings
hand over hand, settled down there.

We'll raise ourselves reaching blossoms,
top-pinnacled blooms, lavender, sweet

melody-minded motion, step after step.
Rhythm walk we wade with, rows

like water,   green, deep.   Fog still suspended
wets grip, khakis,   soaks cotton weave worn

to breathe in fields we'll huff in
another month down the line. When

summer sends us hustling in heat
taking lugs, like tagging games, quicker

rounds than relays. Here, we'll bring
all cylindrical pulls from broader

middles, thickening heights, until
all is gone, cured—then we'll sleep.

THE WAILING ROOM

Always, when it seems just fine,
something stirs against living
steals those we least expect
sometimes murders
comes in fours
fully cornered, squared,
unnaturally man-made tight.

Creeps along skull hunting,
especially those who come with criers
wildly wailing their loss
in deathwatch chambers.
Quiet now, children. Quiet now.

All our grandparents, uncles,
most aunties, some cousins, three brothers—
before they'd even crawled—
friends, some of their kids, brothers,
my one song man—all gone.

Last to go my daughter-in-law's father,
only a few days younger than me he was.
Strong as a bull bear, least what we thought.
Gone, gone.

Both her grandmas,
only grandpa she ever knew,
all gone in a short time.
Gone, gone, gone, she's crying.

My girl, I wish you long life.
Quiet now, they'll hear you.
Some of us see them walking in day,
more at night,   all hesitate knowing
what surrounds us here.
Up to the deathbed, Ravenmocking.
Outside the wailing room, all of you—
Quiet now, children.   Quiet now.

SHAPINGS

I.

A wooden house
rests on her shoulder.
She's making her way up the road
paved with fractured glass,
on a hill steadily rising into
what looks like full mountains.
Buzzards flap like black sheets
in murky sky,
high above frozen peaks, and
around hillsides lined
with bracken ferns.
She's reaching toward greenery
with her shoulders, lunging.
Tension from the structure
is pressing her into a curved shape.
Somewhere a breadboard is
wielded from an oven.
And small coals are falling
on hearth bricks below,
near her feet.
Heat
rushes her face and fingers.
And smell fresh baking aromas
tantalizing in waves.
Slicing, wrapping, and selling
this hot bread,

buys bread for her own brood.
She loses herself
in hot bread whiffs.
Scorching from the oven melts her
into a wrinkled-up form.

II.

What if when, barred with furniture,
the bedroom door
still bulges from blows
landing like bombers on PTS
when the world is at war.
And on the other side
he pounds, pounds,
pounds bloody wrath.
Rage fuming from terrible bottles
somehow impounded
behind his brow.
And then if ampules burst,
shattering, releasing fresh
adrenaline into fists,
she must lean
her back into wood,
hands over ears, numbing.
The quaking from blows
shaking her into a crumpled mess.
Late at night,
a stainless steel shelf
might glide her

back into a drawer.
She could be in a basement
with morticians circulating,
almost arctic breeze blowing.
Their scalpels rocking on tables
wheeled back and forth.
Something spins
gyrates past blue-coated lab
technicians,   green sheet draped nurses.
Everywhere, blood drained bruising
blends with autopsy marks.
Formaldehyde petrifies her soft
flesh into metamorphosed rock.
Not far away, a marble stone
lies snugly between
green grass blades.

III.

She drifts near and
over, plastic daisies   hanging
willows gently dangle rainy leaves,
slicing thick air
where she floats.
White crosses cover, and
gray granite spike
the clearing.
An empty space still lies
next to fresh mound of shoveled earth
beneath double-hearted stone

honoring blissful lovers.
But now she spins away
whirling,
whisking into the next world.
Not even wind can image her
into material shape.

IV.

She is the mother of us all
and the massive fruits of her womb.
While *he* presents the rulers
of the free, dictated, and corporate worlds
all at odds with one another.
As we await rebirth
she holds us.
As we await our fate
she catches us.
As we look for beauty
she comforts us.
As we amass our duty
she pleas with us.
As we hold dear all that is sacred,
all the children of the world
and those that follow,
she reminds us of
what we were
meant to be
and once again offers us
warm bread while

breathing us back to life.
As we await an answer
she loves us.
Mustn't we love her, too?
Not even wind can image her
back into material shape.

AMERICA, I SING YOU BACK

for Phil Young and my father Robert Hedge Coke;
for Whitman and Hughes

America, I sing back. Sing back what sung you in.
Sing back the moment you cherished breath.
Sing you home into yourself and back to reason.

Before America began to sing, I sung her to sleep,
held her cradleboard, wept her into day.
My song gave her creation, prepared her delivery,
held her severed cord beautifully beaded.

My song helped her stand, held her hand for first steps,
nourished her very being, fed her, placed her three sisters strong.
My song comforted her as she battled my reason
broke my long-held footing sure, as any child might do.

As she pushed herself away, forced me to remove myself,
as I cried this country, my song grew roses in each tear's fall.

My blood-veined rivers, painted pipestone quarries
circled canyons, while she made herself maiden fine.

But here I am, here I am, here I remain high on each and every peak,
carefully rumbling her great underbelly, prepared to pour forth singing—

and sing again I will, as I have always done.
Never silenced unless in the company of strangers, singing

the stoic face, polite repose, polite while dancing deep inside, polite
Mother of her world. Sister of myself.

When my song sings aloud again. When I call her back to cradle.
Call her to peer into waters, to behold herself in dark and light,
day and night, call her to sing along, call her to mature, to envision—
then, she will quake herself over. My song will make it so.

When she grows far past her self-considered purpose,
I will sing her back, sing her back. I will sing. Oh I will—I do.
America, I sing back. Sing back what sung you in.

IV

WHERE IT ENDS

for the Marfans

THE LAST HOUSE CREELEY LEFT
for Ben Lerner and Joseph Lease

Days all was away
and the clouds were far off
and the sky was heaven itself,
one wanted to stay.
—FROM "ABSENCE" BY ROBERT CREELEY, *ON EARTH*

Surrounded in
Spring wide windows leveling
horizons, hardwood floors buff
polished, neatly, every angle
cared for, carefully crafted
for a poet to breathe free.

Can the window wear
faces, horizons, lines once
balanced here in temporal
sway, swing out over greater
fields, open, in the open wide
as Texas sky, hovering Marfa
lights? Has he quickened here?

This same bed, same sleep
same chairs, table, bench,
same walls, ceiling, doors,
same windows pull poetry from
deeper place, recessive lean
in the backbelly rumble, crawling

pit, chest, lungs, breath, crawling breath,
spine, shoulders, arms, fingertips to type,
pen, produce some fruited sand plum poetry in
the last house Creeley left.

REDUCTION

All we did was pray for rain
to put the damn thing out.

Couldn't stand the burning
reminding us of the maybe few
thousand in there smoldering.

Or the thousands burned back
Sullivan-Clinton days, dams
lodged, released, anyone left
alive set to flame the next morning.

Damn the blazing.

BREATHING

For weeks we inhaled the dead
scent the same, financier or footman,
and like moths all rested on sills,
searched for light.

BURN

Cattle carcass still steaming,
                       roadside   each way   black,
all we can hope is no human's-gone-pugilistic attitude

shrink-posing for fight when air
                             drains from muscles
through pores evaporating mist in the heat of it

the burnside tangling flesh/ash
                           through whirlwinds
black plumes, threading time disappearing into dark energy

encapsulating West Texas Border Patrol,
                         game wardens, smokejumpers'
interior exit, camouflaged,   must outfox the hustle of fire, bustle

whole depletion into retreat, flee, surrender. Surrender.

Hot metal searing Dad's eye,

                          soldering pipe flash

into sclera surrounding insight.

                          He called to me for water.

I could walk then, but was too

                          young to explain.

Knew the serious nature of it,

                          how to draw water to heal.

Knew how to handle,

                          when passing consumed cattle steaming

their bodies still bearing passing life, still bearing full weight

near normal, flash-burned when

                          they could not escape

tumultuous wind-driven flame. Black clouds on scorched earth

managing weather, amassing AEP

                          restoration process in the lean

charred leg, delineating linear directions, compass needles,

articulating line of duty death,

                          Goins gone, his land still smoking.

The East St. Louis child calling,

"Let me out. Let me out!"

as his grandmother's home buckled inward

too far-gone.

Twice prior, two cousins, sisters lost

in fires years before burn

strangling through the family, bit by bit. As if Missouri tornados

weren't wet enough, the fires fueled there, still hardy, taking.

Up river, season error snowmelt maddening levees,   taking
houses in laps

                              long overgrown, smacking them into tinder

somewhere heated, but now there is the quickened confluence
beating away anything substantial

                              to vehicle flow, with amorous

waves rolling wide, gyrating revolve, pushing, turning twist
into

back into blaze, the only water deep
                              and drifting, not enough hoses
or people to put this out, now another's popped up, maybe more.

By the sixth, caution translates to which way the wind blows,   by
eleventh, homes are temporary, expendable,

                                    nothing matches life.

Massive range-riddling smolder. Tufts turn upward, rise on sweeps.
Glowing bluffs distant horizon, closer
                              burn backs off befuddled

men, women, wishing for work in a heated ten-mile open wide
volcano mouth, held open since seas
                              slid down, lava formed high

not two hundred miles from Carlsbad where evacuations loom,
bats scatter, all wide deep of it,
                              catacombed, put it out north too,

under Los Alamos crazed nuclear weaponry, plutonium storage
experiments hauled over something
                              byway Santa Fe, city

current remnant flagged in trade cloth waving red, yellow flames
on downtown wheeled armadas, honking,
                              "L-e-t u-s o-u-t!" while winds

wind themselves into imperiled   charts, pictographs, cartography cut
loose from Bandolier-sashed mountains,
                              the pockets pushed out

into ashes all around. Now, here, javelinas
                              hurl themselves under
roadside culverts, taking lower pathways from fiery sear.

Remember back on Ridge, fires? Crystal called her sister, Faith said,
                    "The house is gone, all of it."
Sarah standing on top, a black & white in her right palm, her hair

in her left, all of it smoldering.
                    Where's the cat?   My own brother
burning new construction insulation, for the thrill of it; at eight, "Pyromania,"

they said, but never mentioned when he self-immolated at eleven,
no, never gave him that, just coughed
                    away memory of our sister

pouring alcohol on the hard tile, spelling out,
                    "Die Die Die" to
shock us coming home. Kids' stuff.
                    Or, construction workers stubbing

cigarettes into dry grass behind our place,
                    how we burned our rubber
soles stamping while they laughed at us, Mom and Dad burned

their palms putting it out,   ashed,   or her hair shocked that way, white.

Glass bottle fire, smokes up crossroads, no
                              no fiddles found their bow
play   on strings popping alongside road tar
                                        heels, hollowed ditches full

Russian thistles' bitter scorch, flying out
                              skeletal-like, running.
Insides turning out, twisting up like lead turns turning. Rising

mantle vapor smoking sunset, rise,
                              all through night, all through
cooked fields, calves scrambled on, too fast, too fast, the burn. Burn.

We're still missing one hundred twenty-five head
                              from Rock House Fire.
Seventy-four from the leased Poor Farm land. Neighbors keep

a lookout, nothing. Black Angus, aoudad, pronghorns torched up
like marshmallow roasts, giving tongue
                              lapped licks on lips curled

quick in heat.   Twenty-nine special rangers seek the rest, any loose
herds made clean of it. Rustlers, must be.
                              No vultures vortexed

sight overhead, no buzzards' contours,   no, only smoke belies.

Downtown, some fliers offer reward next to a ma and pop chiding
their eldest over dropping lit butt into pathways.

                                    No room for
accidents in *No Country for Old Men.*   No room for it where Woody
wore belts decked out by Graybeal, by

                              Moonlight's best gemstone,
Marfa agate. Too bad the shots didn't display
                                    the cut of them. Real
beauties over sterling silver plate. Now heat plates on low-profile sports

cars tinder prairie grass ignition, cactus wrath. Anything's
at risk; everything's to blame.

                          Flames follow wind the way

water follows wave, over seabed
                          ground pummeled high, mile
high elevation, sure as Denver, but desert scene. Chihuahuan

and Sonoran, now both carry largest wildfires in colonial
history, both heated harder, spreading
                          further, than pictured

in recent times. Everything from Tucson through Texas a rage.

Ladybird's roadside flowers billow dust, chocolate
flowers still scenting straight paths familiar.

                              It's the fury fell
here. Fuming every angle, hopping asphalt,
                              by the time Gage
Holland breaks from roadside rest area, Hwy 90 is shut down clean

to Marfa, no one there holds much hope,
                              Rock House said
to be still smoldering.   It's all without mercy, without peace.

Dreams come easily branded, but no iron rod season's
coming this round. Come easily into

                    infused chicken   games,

forearms stubbed, spoons cooked in dosage blues, shooting
burns, shoot-up euphoria, hero flying

                    through blistered skies,
they called it horse at import, now horses shot, nine of them.
Nerves so frayed teakettle copper melts blue,

                    then white, ash

covered the electric burner on stove range, while the range
outside roared, spat sideways onto

                    roofs, roads, ranches.

Population too sparse here for national concern, no, though
public radio does spare lives nearby, maybe

                                          our own, measly thrill

a bitter bitter thing in coverage accolades, but dammit they do
deserve attention, we depend on them.

                                           Give them glory, we'll

share in it, same face, Border Patrol/Walk In, all phoenix rise,
nothing sheared shares grace,

                                           black peel crusts everything,

surviving's the only reason. Look at it, gone. No fire climax
pines here to justify so much loss,

                                           rebirth here, a fought thing.

Mr. Spanish buried ceremonially in shoebox, under glory, flagpoled,
                                          each niña entered escuela.

It's rough country. Aftermath don't add up.
                                        Logic's subjective.
That's life out here, not much gussy ghost propositions. Trains

all that ever run on time, rest of the clockwork's *when it need
be* business. Rain's only thing missing.
                                        When it teases,

lightning sparks whatever's left, six sparks spread within an evening.
By morning smoke's on the plate again.
                                        Coexistence only calm.

We expect plunther, plunther along the world's edge, horizon.
One day a rim fire burns so great its whirl will create weather,

                pattern vortices tilt horizontal to vertical, hurling

branch, limb, whatever fills to vorticity. Scorched pathways leaving earth.

All roads travel onward, until they end.

Everything ends in time.

Everything temporary. An eternal fire holds itself, only in heat,

fuel, oxygen, triangulate combustion,

tetrahedral support planes

existence, life spark, yet fire has been carried, cultivated, cured

since first fire. It's log bundle, hollowed, fed.

He fed the first from his pickup on I-44. Tossed the news out his window,

flaming until half of Luther

left Oklahoma in fury so hot, all it left was white ash, the whole of it

under skies dark with night

shining proof of other worlds. Orion holding up east. The gleam of it maddening.

Stars surely shine. Sun's running sky each morning.
Sirius still rounds night except

for seventy days or so.

Always will. Stardust precedes Earth.

Dust here kicks up heavy, towered seventy feet high
in Lubbock years back.

                              High in Arizona now, where

Wallow breaks records like gangbusters.

                             Mainstreamers
picking up haboob as if comprehension made it new.

Predate dust. You can't. Dust has been and rises when-
ever wind wills.

                         Gusts a given out here.

Where a heat plate scrapes grass like armadillo shell
tears into straw with friction, sparks it,

                          whole thing burns

bright, spreads for miles in short order. Spreads for miles.

People unable to move through it, leave everything they love, hope
until return, then weep. Like the mother

                          whose kids shared our

school. One tied to the couch and burned alive after Demerol
                                downed him there. Bad deal.
                                Bad deal all over. Drug wars
never won. Border blasting happening here.
                                Bad deal all over.

SBI burned down the shooting gallery back when. Now
'tis anyone's game, gamble,

                          crap shoot, loosing lives like

spit on clay, baked hard, broken.

                          What's the seed of it?   Crack?

Char rounds out horizon now,

                              used to be shadows. Tall
men in saddles shifting through, now shadow men unsaddled

blow away in wind on giant flat.

                                  Secrets untold shudder
what should be proper, what should be here, gone. Gone.

Char brings looseness, holds memory intangible, blackened
earth,   its own beauty, not hollow
                              but kept there. In

evening, vultures scan space, seeking remnant, passing cranes feast
on roasted grasshoppers, crickets, larva.
                              In morning, phoenix

rises through community sight, open to opportunity, lamenting.
We come here hoping for more,
                              knowing nothing surprises

those who present hope. What is hope?   Feel fortune?
Opportunity? Grace?

In the meantime, all wade through ashes, in a place ash
turned to stone when volcanoes

                              came up from the sea floor,
now high desert, what's left of it, caldera.

                              Putting down the suffering,
the day's work. Beloved and betrothed—horse, cattle, goat.

The chickens hold a roost with their burnt legs, they go as well
to wayside memory, now asunder,

                              memory, like the paisano,
skipping in, out, walking upward, falling,

                              bird, fountain motion,
moving.

                          We were born here, someone mentions.

We don't know when fire will still, when embers left end themselves,
nor when rain will visit, come to renew,

                                    to free us from burn, from danger.

Nor do we know what caused this end, the timing of a heat plate on long
grass, the nearness of glass to blade in sunlight.

                                 The year of the drought,

though some speculate larger cycles,

                                  the roundabout here is intangible.

Nor do we offer ideas, unless plied with cold lager in the heat here, or

in evenings laid out under fiery stars still gleaming, always lighting
pathways we lean toward in nighttime escapes,

                                  to towns down the road.

No we don't know. All we know is we are not alone
and yet we are and everything is subject to fire,

                                  even water leaves

in heated paths. What we don't know we don't search for, nor do we
attempt to understand. No, we take it.

                                  Deal with it. We muster.

We move through the crust salvaging pieces, we are salvagers, moving
through the heat, lifting recognizable source,

                                       lifting permanence

from tempered time. Lifting home. We tote burned wire, curled into sphere
like story, surround light with it,

                                       harness energy and plug it in until

spherical globes rekindle Marfa fires once surrounding livestock, now bordering
glow, it is the strand we fill, the obligation,

                                       remaking stuff from cinder.

Remaking.

Remaking.
      Twins we carried then laid.
                    One light, one fire.   Do they rest?
Do they feel this burden? The melting iron, wire,
                            shifting wind funneling

them across prairie in winding plumes, are they turning?

                  What of the way
we embraced to conceive them?   Held there like satchels beaded

in cedar spring holding floral bursts.   In dense trees, hills,   waterways
we come from,   the kneel there
                when we bury, bring them gifts, make offerings.

In the burn of your brow, when you hastened, did you think before belting
me? Conceive intent?
                What were you, but burning?

                What were you,   but burning?

Yet, fire is the birth of life, the spark there and we
                                    were with spark, ignited.
My life emptied into the banks below mounds they now lay within. They

were within me, now within our mother.

                              I sometimes long to lie there but

I, too, muster.

You,   long gone to other worlds,

not over there, but wandering spark,

burn.

CODA

HARP STRINGS

Sweet rain on old growth sweeps past in fanning sheets,
this morning each veil brings joy, like someone strumming
mist releasing song, falling to branch above hummingbird
dashing in, out, grabbing nectar in the wet, wet, music.
Dashing in, out, grabbing nectar in the wet, wet, music.
Mist releasing song, falling to branch above hummingbird
this morning, each veil brings joy, like someone strumming.
Sweet rain on old growth sweeps past in fanning sheets.

NOTES

This book contains references to cultural ideology, cosmogony, scientific phenomena, and historical and political events, as well as multiple inclusions of botanical, zoological, and geological terminology. I believe most of these references are readily available for research and hope to lead the reader to discover more, extending the work of the poems. Some cultural complexities will have an aesthetic effect on the audience, while understanding the deeper encoded properties will resonate more with those more familiar with the culture base (as in any world literature). Additionally, I hope these few notes will serve some use to the reader.

STREAMING

- Dog Road: The Milky Way.
- Darkening Land: A place of afterlife for humans and animals.
- Cygnus: A seasonally demonstrative constellation.
- Northern Cross: A prominent asterism featured in Cygnus that is also known as the backbone of the Milky Way. As Cygnus moves with the seasons, the shape of the Northern Cross within it seems to peer down, like a long bird looking over the horizon to the west toward the Darkening Land. The bird formations migrate west seasonally.
- Albireo: The fifth-brightest star in Cygnus. It is actually a binary star, where the brighter star is a golden yellow and the dimmer, a deep, rich blue.
- tutsi bowl: A bowl, or pocket, spun of spider silk that Spider wears on her back to carry great things (like fire).

DRUNK BUTTERFLIES

- kamama: Butterfly.

HEROES

- Reference to an event on March 14, 2013, at Falls Park on the Big Sioux River in Sioux Falls, South Dakota. Garret Wallace, a white six-year-old, fell into the falls. His sister Madison, a white sixteen-year-old, jumped in to try to save him. Lyle Eagle Tail, a twenty-eight-year-old Lakota—and a complete stranger to them both—jumped in to try to save them. The boy survived, and the other two drowned. It was both an act of heroism and a supreme sacrifice.

PANDO/PANDO

- Pando, the Trembling Giant Aspen: A giant indigenous North American clonal colony. At eighty thousand years old and weighing six million kilograms, it is the heaviest living organism (and among the oldest) on Earth and was once thought to be a whole forest of individual, separate growth (rather than a single living organism sharing a massive underground root system) in the Fishlake National Forest in Utah.

- Pando, massacre: Also known as El Porvenir Massacre. The deadly ambush occurring September 11, 2008, was on Indigenous community members (including students) who were supporters of President Evo Morales, the first Indigenous president—and an Indigenous giant—of Bolivia.

SWARMING

- The invasion of Iraq in 2003.

HIBAKUSHA

- Hibakusha: Literally translates to explosion-affected people. The term refers specifically to the survivors of the atomic bombings of Hiroshima and Nagasaki.

STEEL

- Aftermath, September 11, 2001, New York City.

STORY

- Aftermath, September 11, 2001, New York City.

SEARCHING GROUND

- Aftermath, September 11, 2001, New York City.

1973

- Reference to the Wounded Knee incident, a seventy-one day occupation, standoff, and protest of civil and human rights violations on people of the Oglala Sioux Tribe by the Guardians of the Oglala Nation (GOON) political force and the United States government. Local youth, and adults were in bunkers with leaders from outside the area who came in to answer a call for support. Many of the participants lost family members to the ongoing brutality by GOON forces. In the aftermath of the protest, the GOONs killed about sixty more people, and multitudes of others were injured. Those locals that were teenagers while protesting are in their fifties today, if they survived.

- leciya o iyokipi: over here / (the people) we are happy—pleased with something pleasant (in this case in the afterlife, as a double entendre).

SOLAR FLARES

- Reference to the K-12 teacher protests February 14, 2011, in Madison, Wisconsin, and the powerful X2.2-class solar flare occurring the same date.

- *Which Way Home*: A documentary following unaccompanied child migrants.

FIRST MORNING

- The March 2010 Split This Rock festival in Washington, DC.

BARRIO TRICENTENARIO, PLAZA DE BANDERAS

- References places where community people were criminally executed and murdered, and a bombing of a Botero sculpture as an act of violence upon the poetry festival of Medellin, Colombia, held annually for peace, and where I have read on multiple occasions.

NIÑO DE LA CALLE

- Niño(s) de la Calle: Term for street children in Medellin, Colombia.

DUBLIN CROSSING

- *The Blue Boy:* A magnificent play I attended as part of the Ulster Bank Dublin Theater Festival regarding the horrendous abuse in residential schools in Ireland, and a ghost story of a boy who perished in unknown circumstances.

- The Magdalene Laundries: Asylums where unwed mothers and their children were taken, treated as criminals, kept, starved, and abused in Ireland.

- Also relates to crimes by the Church on Indigenous peoples across the waters in the Americas, in this case in northern North America, beginning with the Black Robes.

WAS MORNING CALL

- Qahweh: Coffee.

- chayi: Tea.

- Arabi: Arabic.

HATCHLINGS

- Anitsata: Choctaw.

- Wampano/Quiripi: A language spoken by Indigenous peoples from western Connecticut and Long Island.

- Mercy Nonsuch: The last full-blood Nehantic.

- Borrelia burgdorferi: The causative agent of Lyme disease, which is spread by deer ticks.

- Little Deer: Punished hunters that killed without need or mercy (and without prayer for mercy from the deer) with inflamed joints, as in rheumatoid arthritis and Lyme disease.

WEATHERBAND/FM/AM

- The tornados on May 20, 2013, in Moore, Oklahoma, and surrounding areas.

WE WERE IN A WORLD

- Birling: Spinning.

- Boson: A photon or other subatomic particle with zero or integral spin.

- Boson melts: My (coined) reference to Higgs boson (aka the God particle, a boson with no spin, electric charge, or color change; also, a particle that is very unstable), the Large Hadron Collider, and the quantum melting and absence of Bose-Einstein condensation in two-dimensional vortex matter, as demonstrated in an experiment by Jairo Sinova, C. B. Hanna, and A. H. MacDonald, who estimate "the boson filling factor at which the vortex lattice melts are consistent with recent exact-diagonalization calculations" ("Quantum Melting and Absence of Bose-Einstein Condensation in Two-Dimensional Vortex Matter," *Physical Review Letters*, no. 89 [2002]).

- The reference here also relates to fundamental forces of nature, symmetry, chaos, and creation, and the possibility of breaks in these laws. The irony in the seeking.

- Oraliteratures: Indigenous scholar term, especially common in South America.

IN THE YEAR 513 PC

- References to multiple climate change occurrences—and Indigenous prophesies regarding their coming—with the arrival of Europeans upon the Americas.

TWISTIN' THE NIGHT AWAY

- Tornados in the Oklahoma City area, May 2013.
- Deep Deuce: Ralph Waldo Ellison's Oklahoma City homeplace.

THEN

- The Black Blizzard of May 9, 1934 (other Dust Bowl poems follow in tribute to my father, a survivor).

RAINMAKER

- This poem relies on cultural and familial memory and knowledge while considering the complications faced in climate shifts, resource depletion, and exterminations of beings necessary to Indigenous livelihood and culture, from North America down to the Orinoco Delta in Venezuela, while noticing similarities between, and indicating possible kinships with, Indigenous peoples in each region, and renewing reliance on traditional beingness in the world gone awry.

TOBACCO RISE

- Visqueen: A heavy plastic used in plant beds to shield infant plants, in this case the tobacco seedlings. I was a tobacco sharecropper in my teens and early adulthood in North Carolina. My father had been a migrant and local cotton picker, with his cousins working in indigo, as demonstrated in two previous poems.

REDUCTION

- References the largest expedition ever mounted upon American Indians at that time (1779). Tribes were under treaty with the British Empire. The "patriots" were British as well. The Haudenosaunee suffered and were starved, and many expired from floods and fires caused by the expedition. Others died as the result of a steady onslaught under Washington, who called for the Six Nations' towns to be completely destroyed, and that no overture of peace be heard by the troops before total ruinment was achieved. This was an American holocaust and involved fiery death.

BREATHING

- Aftermath, September 11, 2001, New York City.

BURN

- This poem stems from the multiple Marfa fires of 2011. It references many other personal, historical, familial, and newsworthy events that were intensified in the midst of the heat, climate change, and catastrophe.

HARP STRINGS

- Written during a 2010 residency in old growth at the Dragonfly Eyes National Science Foundation Research Field Symposium in H.J. Andrews Experimental Forest, Oregon.

ACKNOWLEDGMENTS

Some versions of these poems first appeared in editions of *Anti-;* *Asian American Literary Review; Black Renaissance Noire; Caliban Online; Connecticut Review; Connotation Press: An Online Artifact; Cream City Review; The Ecopoetry Anthology; Future Earth Magazine; Gargoyle Magazine; Ghost Town; A Harvest of Words: Contemporary South Dakota Poetry; Hick Poetics; Kenyon Review; Love Rise Up: Poems of Social Justice, Protest, and Hope; Malpais Review; Many Mountains Moving; Naropa Summer Magazine; Native Realities; New Mexico Poetry Review; North American Review; North Carolina Literary Review;* North Carolina Arts Council Website; *Paddlefish; Passages North; Political Affairs; Poets Against the War; Prometeo; Sentence; Sing: Poetry of the Indigenous Americas; South Dakota Review; Sou' wester;* Split This Rock; *Talking Stick Amerind;* United Nations: Poems for Peace; *The Untidy Season: An Anthology of Nebraska Women Poets; Waxwings; Weber: The Contemporary West; The Willow's Whisper: A Transatlantic Compilation of Poetry from Ireland and Native America; Wingbeats II; Women Write Resistance: Poets Resist Gender Violence;* and *Yellow Medicine Review;*

were recorded for entities such as From the Fish House, PennSound, Poets House, the Naropa Archive, the Poetry Center, the Poetry Project, *Harry's House Archive,* and for the 2014 *Harry's House, Vol. II* album with Ambrose Bye for Fast Speaking Music;

composed within the Red Dust Project;

printed as broadsides in *P3* shows at the Washington Pavilion;

included in the special edition *Burn* for MadHat Press;

& recorded & released on the *Streaming* album with the trio Rd Klā (rdkla.com) for Long Person (Yvwi Gvnahita) Records.

Thank you to Drue Heinz & Hawthornden Castle
for the generation of this collection.

Thank you to the Weymouth Center &
Kimmel Harding Nelson Center for additional time.

Thank you to the Lannan Foundation; completion of this book
was made possible by residency at Marfa.

———

For Quincy & Margaret Porter Troupe, Diane Zephier, Matthew Shenoda, Juan Felipe Herrera, Sherwin Bitsui, Adrian Matejka, Jodi Melamed, Lee Ann Roripaugh, Jan Beatty, Wang Ping, Cristina Eisenberg, Kim Blaeser, Thea Temple, Craig Santos Perez, Brandy Nālani McDougall, Kaikainaliʻi, Paula Nelson, and Kimberly Becker, whose friendship, kindness, collaboration, and care are deeply appreciated & essential;

to Kelvyn Bell & Laura Ortman for the genius sound art & camaraderie;

to John Carolos Perea & Jimmy Biala for the sweet sounds & smooth collaboration;

to Dustin Mater for the fierce beauty and Shane Brown for exquisite work & exceptional presence;

to Nancy Morejon, Sonja Sanchez, Marc Vincenz, Marilyn Lone Hill, Bill Wetzel, Jennifer Foerster, Marilyn Nelson, Kim Blaeser, Anne Waldman, Arthur Sze, Natasha Trethewey, Karenne Wood, Jon Davis, Jill O'Mahony, Ted Kooser, Sydney Brown, Royce Sharp, Jeffrey Palmer, James Payne, Crisosto Apache,

LeAnne Howe, Ibrahim Nasrallah, Chadwick Allen, Susan Bernardin, Ceca Cooper, Phil Young, Joy Castro, Bojan Louis, Jack Collom, Bobbie Louise Hawkins, Linda Rodriguez, Penelope Kelsey, Cari Carpenter, Molly McGlennen, and Connie Walstrom, for support, inspiration, collaboration, and camaraderie.

This book pays tribute to Mary Maria, Charley Patton, Harry Partch, Lou Reed, Amiri Baraka, Jayne Cortez, Walt Whitman, Langston Hughes, Ralph Waldo Ellison, Bob Creeley, Jack Myers, Ivy Lucy, Anselm Hollo, Charlie Hill, Milton Apache, Lyle Eagle Tail, and Madison Leigh Wallace;

to those suffering fires, floods, tornadoes, quakes, dust, and great storms of injustices throughout all these days;

is with love for all, especially Travis, Vaughan, Hazel, Deja, Andrez, Alice, Aariana, Skuya, Edward, Edwin, Dec, Caesar, Johnny, Sawin, Sara, Sienna, Sam, Athena, Malcolm, Benjamin, and all the kids—thank you all for your presence;

for Stephanie;

for Randye & Andrea Beth, and Jay;
for Caroline, Molly, Amelia, Elizabeth, Erika, Julie, and Linda;

for Allan Kornblum, Chris Fischbach, Anitra Budd, and Coffee House for sustaining the life of the work;

for all the supporters of the Red Dust Project
& those poems in this mix;

for my father, a wonderful human being,
& in memory of my mother, Hazel,
& everyone before.

COFFEE HOUSE PRESS

The mission of Coffee House Press is to publish exciting, vital, and enduring authors of our time; to delight and inspire readers; to contribute to the cultural life of our community; and to enrich our literary heritage. By building on the best traditions of publishing and the book arts, we produce books that celebrate imagination, innovation in the craft of writing, and the many authentic voices of the American experience.

Visit us at coffeehousepress.org.

FUNDER ACKNOWLEDGMENTS

Coffee House Press is an independent, nonprofit literary publisher. All of our books, including the one in your hands, are made possible through the generous support of grants and donations from corporate giving programs, state and federal support, family foundations, and the many individuals that believe in the transformational power of literature. We receive major operating support from Amazon, the Bush Foundation, the McKnight Foundation, the National Endowment for the Arts—a federal agency, and Target. This activity is made possible by the voters of Minnesota through a Minnesota State Arts Board Operating Support grant, thanks to a legislative appropriation from the arts and cultural heritage fund.

Coffee House Press receives additional support from many anonymous donors; the Alexander Family Fund; the Elmer L. & Eleanor J. Andersen Foundation; the David & Mary Anderson

Family Foundation; the W. and R. Bernheimer Family Foundation; the E. Thomas Binger and Rebecca Rand Fund of the Minneapolis Foundation; Bookmobile; the Patrick and Aimee Butler Family Foundation; the Buuck Family Foundation; the Carolyn Foundation; Dorsey & Whitney Foundation; Fredrikson & Byron, P.A.; the Jerome Foundation; the Lenfestey Family Foundation; the Mead Witter Foundation; the Nash Foundation; the Rehael Fund of the Minneapolis Foundation; the Schwab Charitable Fund; Schwegman, Lundberg, Woessner & Kluth, P.A.; Penguin Group; the Private Client Reserve of US Bank; the Archie D. & Bertha H. Walker Foundation; the Wells Fargo Foundation of Minnesota; and the Woessner Freeman Family Foundation.

THE PUBLISHERS CIRCLE
OF COFFEE HOUSE PRESS

The Publishers Circle is an exclusive group of individuals who make significant contributions to Coffee House Press's annual giving campaign. Understanding that a strong financial base is necessary for the press to meet the challenges and opportunities that arise each year, this group plays a crucial part in the success of our mission.

Coffee House Press believes that American literature should be as diverse as America itself. Known for consistently championing authors whose work challenges cultural and aesthetic norms, we believe their books deserve space in the marketplace of ideas.

Publishing literature has never been an easy business, and publishing literature that truly takes risks is a cause we believe is worthy of significant support. We ask you to join us today in helping to ensure the future of Coffee House Press.

—THE PUBLISHERS CIRCLE MEMBERS
OF COFFEE HOUSE PRESS

PUBLISHERS CIRCLE MEMBERS INCLUDE:

Many Anonymous Donors

Mr. & Mrs. Rand L. Alexander

Suzanne Allen

Patricia Beithon

Bill Berkson & Connie Lewallen

Claire Casey

Louise Copeland

Jane Dalrymple-Hollo

Mary Ebert & Paul Stembler

Chris Fischbach & Katie Dublinski

Katharine Freeman

Sally French

Jocelyn Hale & Glenn Miller

Roger Hale & Nor Hall

Jeffrey Hom

Kenneth Kahn & Susan Dicker

Kenneth Koch Literary Estate

Stephen & Isabel Keating

Allan & Cinda Kornblum

Kathryn & Dean Koutsky

Leslie Larson Maheras

Jim & Susan Lenfestey

Sarah Lutman

Carol & Aaron Mack

George Mack

Joshua Mack

Gillian McCain

Mary & Malcolm McDermid

Sjur Midness & Briar Andresen

Peter Nelson & Jennifer Swenson

E. Thomas Binger and Rebecca Rand Fund
of the Minneapolis Foundation

Jeffrey Sugerman & Sarah Schultz

Nan Swid

Patricia Tilton

Stu Wilson & Melissa Barker

Warren Woessner & Iris Freeman

Margaret Wurtele

For more information about the Publishers Circle and other ways
to support Coffee House Press books, authors, and activities,
please visit coffeehousepress.org/support or contact us at:
info@coffeehousepress.org.

COLOPHON

Streaming was designed at Coffee House Press, in the historic Grain Belt Brewery's Bottling House near downtown Minneapolis. The text is set in Garamond.

ALLISON ADELLE HEDGE COKE is an American Book Award–winning author. Her previous poetry volumes include *Dog Road Woman, Off-Season City Pipe, Blood Run,* and *Burn.* She wrote *Rock Ghost, Willow, Deer,* a memoir, and is the editor of *Sing: Poetry of the Indigenous Americas, Effigies,* and *Effigies II.* She currently serves as a distinguished writer at the University of Hawai'i at Mānoa. Hedge Coke came of age working fields, factories, and waters and is currently at work on a film, *Red Dust: the dirty thirties,* chronicling mixed-blood and Native life.